FRANCIS FRITH'S
SOMERSET
LIVING MEMORIES

BRIAN PEARCE is Research and Information Officer for Exmoor National Park Authority, and spends much time researching facts and figures about that area and the West Country as a whole. He has an extensive knowledge of local history, and maintains a photographic archive. In addition, he is a freelance writer, photographer, lecturer and guide. He has written a variety of books on West Country themes, including Francis Frith's *Minehead* and *Padstow*. He has contributed many walks and trails throughout the West Country to national publications, and he writes regular articles about local food.

SOMERSET
LIVING MEMORIES

BRIAN PEARCE

First published in the United Kingdom in 2004 by
Frith Book Company Ltd

Hardback Edition 2004
ISBN 1-85937-537-5

British Library Cataloguing in Publication Data

Francis Frith's Somerset - Living Memories
Brian Pearce

Frith Book Company Ltd
Frith's Barn, Teffont,
Salisbury, Wiltshire SP3 5QP
Tel: +44 (0) 1722 716 376
Email: info@francisfrith.co.uk
www.francisfrith.co.uk

Printed and bound in Great Britain

Front Cover: **MINEHEAD,** *The Bristol Queen in the Harbour c1960* M84196
Frontispiece:**BLUE ANCHOR,** *The Beach* B124047

*The colour-tinting is for illustrative purposes only, and is not intended
to be historically accurate*

AS WITH ANY HISTORICAL DATABASE THE FRITH ARCHIVE IS CONSTANTLY
BEING CORRECTED AND IMPROVED, AND THE PUBLISHERS WOULD
WELCOME INFORMATION ON OMISSIONS OR INACCURACIES

CONTENTS

FRANCIS FRITH
VICTORIAN PIONEER

FRANCIS FRITH, founder of the world-famous photographic archive, was a complex and multi-talented man. A devout Quaker and a highly successful Victorian businessman, he was philosophical by nature and pioneering in outlook.

By 1855 he had already established a wholesale grocery business in Liverpool, and sold it for the astonishing sum of £200,000, which is the equivalent today of over £15,000,000. Now a very rich man, he was able to indulge his passion for travel. As a child he had pored over travel books written by early explorers, and his fancy and imagination had been stirred by family holidays to the sublime mountain regions of Wales and Scotland. 'What lands of spirit-stirring and enriching scenes and places!' he had written. He was to return to these scenes of grandeur in later years to 'recapture the thousands of vivid and tender memories', but with a different purpose. Now in his thirties, and captivated by the new science of photography, Frith set out on a series of pioneering journeys up the Nile and to the Near East that occupied him from 1856 unti 1860.

INTRIGUE AND EXPLORATION

These far-flung journeys were packed with intrigue and adventure. In his life story, written when he was sixty-three, Frith tells of being held captive by bandits, and of fighting 'an awful midnight battle to the very point of surrender with a deadly pack of hungry, wild dogs'. Wearing flowing Arab costume, Frith arrived at Akaba by camel sixty years before Lawrence of Arabia, where he encountered 'desert princes and rival sheikhs, blazing with jewel-hilted swords'.

He was the first photographer to venture beyond the sixth cataract of the Nile. Africa was still the mysterious 'Dark Continent', and Stanley and Livingstone's historic meeting was a decade into the future. The conditions for picture taking confound belief. He laboured for hours in his wicker dark-room in the sweltering heat of the desert, while the volatile chemicals fizzed dangerously in their trays. Back in London he exhibited his photographs and was 'rapturously cheered' by members of the Royal Society. His reputation as a photographer was made overnight.

VENTURE OF A LIFE-TIME

Characteristically, Frith quickly spotted the opportunity to create a new business as a specialist publisher of photographs. He lived in an era of immense and sometimes violent change. For the poor in the early part of Victoria's reign work was exhausting and the hours long, and people had precious little free time to enjoy themselves. Most people had no transport other than a cart or gig at their disposal, and rarely

travelled far beyond the boundaries of their own town or village. However, by the 1870s the railways had threaded their way across the country, and Bank Holidays and half-day Saturdays had been made obligatory by Act of Parliament. All of a sudden the working man and his family were able to enjoy days out and see a little more of the world.

With typical business acumen, Francis Frith foresaw that these new tourists would enjoy having souvenirs to commemorate their days out. In 1860 he married Mary Ann Rosling and set out on a new career: his aim was to photograph every city, town and village in Britain. For the next thirty years he travelled the country by train and by pony and trap, producing fine photographs of seaside resorts and beauty spots that were keenly bought by millions of Victorians. These prints were painstakingly pasted into family albums and pored over during the dark nights of winter, rekindling precious memories of summer excursions.

THE RISE OF FRITH & CO

Frith's studio was soon supplying retail shops all over the country. To meet the demand he gathered about him a small team of photographers, and published the work of independent artist-photographers of the calibre of Roger Fenton and Francis Bedford. In order to gain some understanding of the scale of Frith's

business one only has to look at the catalogue issued by Frith & Co in 1886: it runs to some 670 pages, listing not only many thousands of views of the British Isles but also many photographs of most European countries, and China, Japan, the USA and Canada - note the sample page shown on page 9 from the hand-written Frith & Co ledgers recording the pictures. By 1890 Frith had created the greatest specialist photographic publishing company in the world, with over 2,000 sales outlets - more than the combined number that Boots and WH Smith have today! The picture on the next page shows the Frith & Co display board at Ingleton in the Yorkshire Dales (left of window). Beautifully constructed with a mahogany frame and gilt inserts, it could display up to a dozen local scenes.

POSTCARD BONANZA

The ever-popular holiday postcard we know today took many years to develop. In 1870 the Post Office issued the first plain cards, with a pre-printed stamp on one face. In 1894 they allowed other publishers' cards to be sent through the mail with an attached adhesive halfpenny stamp. Demand grew rapidly, and in 1895 a new size of postcard was permitted called the court card, but there was little room for illustration. In 1899, a year after Frith's death, a new card measuring 5.5 x 3.5 inches became the standard format, but it was not until 1902 that the divided back came into being, so that the address and message could be on one face and a full-size illustration on the other. Frith & Co were in the vanguard of postcard development: Frith's sons Eustace and Cyril continued their father's monumental task, expanding the number of views offered to the public and recording more and more places in Britain, as the coasts and countryside were opened up to mass travel.

Francis Frith had died in 1898 at his villa in Cannes, his great project still growing. The archive he created continued in business for another seventy years. By 1970 it contained over a third of a million pictures showing 7,000 British towns and villages.

FRANCIS FRITH'S LEGACY

Frith's legacy to us today is of immense significance and value, for the magnificent archive of evocative photographs he created provides a unique record of change in the cities, towns and villages throughout Britain over a century and more. Frith and his fellow studio photographers revisited locations many times down the years to update their views, compiling for us an enthralling and colourful pageant of British life and character.

We are fortunate that Frith was dedicated to recording the minutiae of everyday life. For it is this sheer wealth of visual data, the painstaking chronicle of changes in dress, transport, street layouts, buildings, housing, engineering and landscape that captivates us so much today. His remarkable images offer us a powerful link with the past and with the lives of our ancestors.

THE VALUE OF THE ARCHIVE TODAY

Computers have now made it possible for Frith's many thousands of images to be accessed almost instantly. Frith's images are increasingly used as visual resources, by social historians, by researchers into genealogy and ancestry, by architects and town planners, and by teachers involved in local history projects.

In addition, the archive offers every one of us an opportunity to examine the places where we and our families have lived and worked down the years. Highly successful in Frith's own era, the archive is now, a century and more on, entering a new phase of popularity. Historians consider the Francis Frith Collection to be of prime national importance. It is the only archive of its kind remaining in private ownership. Francis Frith's archive is now housed in an historic timber barn in the beautiful village of Teffont in Wiltshire. Its founder would not recognize the archive office as it is today. In place of the many thousands of dusty boxes containing glass plate negatives and an all-pervading odour of photographic chemicals, there are now ranks of computer screens. He would be amazed to watch his images travelling round the world at unimaginable speeds through internet lines.

The archive's future is both bright and exciting. Francis Frith, with his unshakeable belief in making photographs available to the greatest number of people, would undoubtedly approve of what is being done today with his lifetime's work. His photographs depicting our shared past are now bringing pleasure and enlightenment to millions around the world a century and more after his death.

SOMERSET
AN INTRODUCTION

IT would be difficult to find a more diverse county than Somerset. There can be few greater contrasts than in the short drive from the acid moors of Exmoor to the limestone hills of Mendip. In between are the forested Brendon Hills, the sheltered Vale of Taunton Deane, the heath-topped ridge of the Quantocks and the low-lying Levels and Moors, from which protrude the Polden Hills, Brent Knoll and Glastonbury Tor, once rising like islands from a vast mere.

The name 'Somerset' is a translation by the Saxons of the name of the Celtic tribe who were there before them, and it means 'people of the summer lands'. 'Sete' means summer pasture, and the marshes around Somerton were used by early Saxon migrants for summer grazing of sheep.

WELLS, *The Market Place c1960* W47052

Somerset grew prosperous with the woollen industry in medieval times. This prosperity funded a spate of church rebuilding in the Perpendicular style of architecture. The local lord of the manor would fund the chancel and family chapels, whilst the parishioners would fund other parts. Travelling bands of masons would go from village to village, and there would be local rivalry in building the most beautiful churches. The older towers were above the crossing at the centre of the churches, but new towers were added at the west end, where they could be made taller. The towers were built in several stages, each with pinnacles and buttresses, and the final stage included intricate tracery in the belfry lights. This became known as the Somerset style.

Local government reorganisation in 1974 reduced the area of the county and divided the remainder into four districts. The most densely populated and wealthiest parts went to the new county of Avon, itself now split into smaller unitary authorities. Somerset became a smaller county based on a rural economy. However, whilst the agricultural element of the economy has declined, in recent years Somerset has seen considerable inward migration of people both for retirement and to work in small industries. Somerset towns were once known for their produce: Taunton and Chard for textiles and clothing; Bridgwater for brick making and engineering; Crewkerne for rope making; Yeovil for glove making; and mid-Somerset for shoe making and leather goods.

MINEHEAD, *The Harbour c1950* M84107

Whilst these traditional industries have all but disappeared, new industries have taken their place: business services in Taunton; food packaging in Bridgwater; printing in Frome; and aerospace in Yeovil. Food processing has continued, with Somerset cider and cheese still being popular. There are many new food products, however, and vineyards are now scattered throughout the county.

Tourism has become an increasing part of the economy. The construction of the M5 in the 1970s did not give the industry quite the boost that was expected: it coincided with the increase in popularity of package holidays abroad, and traditional tourist resorts such as Weston-super-Mare and Clevedon declined. However, the West Country remains the most popular tourist destination for British people, with Somerset playing an important part. 1950s holiday camps at Brean, Burnham-on-Sea and Minehead have kept pace with the times and are still very popular.

Somerset's gardens are of much interest to visitors. The county has had the attentions of well-known garden designers, including Gertrude Jekyll and Sir Edwin Lutyens at Hestercombe; Margery Fish at East Lambrook Manor; and Penelope Hobhouse at more modern gardens. There are many other famous people with Somerset connections. Among the historical figures are the legendary King Arthur, King Alfred, Sir George Williams (founder of the YMCA), Admiral Robert Blake, St Dunstan, Captain Robert Scott the explorer and Lord Trenchard (founder of the RAF). It has many associations with artists.

WESTON-SUPER-MARE, *The Grand Pier c1955* W69079

Among the writers who have lived here are Arthur C Clarke, Evelyn Waugh, Henry Fielding, John Steinbeck, Margaret Drabble and Terry Pratchett. Somerset poets have included Samuel Taylor Coleridge, T S Eliot and William Wordsworth. Actors, musicians and impresarios have included Charles Dance, Frankie Howerd, Georgie Fame, Sir Cameron Macintosh and Sir Henry Irving.

This book has been divided along district and unitary authority boundaries. The photographs follow an imaginary tour of the county from west to east, travelling in that direction through each district.

BLUE ANCHOR, *The Beach c1955* B124047

WEST SOMERSET

▲ **PORLOCK WEIR,** *The Harbour c1960* P721045

Here the cottages at Turkey (the Quay) are seen from the former fish market. The current lock gates, erected in 1913, held back water for unloading ships at low tide. They are now used to sluice the channel clear of pebbles. Coal and limestone were once brought from Wales, and pit props were sent there.

◄ **PORLOCK WEIR,** *The Village Shop c1960* P721081

Porlock Weir is named from the old fish weir or trap on the beach. As fishing declined, the fishermen's wives sold teas from their cottages. The shops survive, and the fishing stores and salting sheds to the left are now craft workshops.

WEST SOMERSET is the poorest district in Somerset in terms of its economy, but the wealthiest in its scenery. The ridges of old red Devonian sandstones and shales are divided by vales of new red sandstones, giving rich red soils. These stones are used in the buildings of Minehead, the district's main tourist resort. Older buildings are often of coursed rubble, rendered and whitewashed, and red Bridgwater tiles are common.

The Vale of Porlock is noted for its beautiful thatched cottages preserved on the National Trust's vast Holnicote Estate, which rises to Dunkery Beacon, at 1,705ft Somerset's highest point. The estate became the core of Exmoor National Park, created in 1954, when the Quantocks became one of the country's first Areas of Outstanding Natural Beauty. Both Exmoor and the Quantocks have high, rounded hills, colourful heaths, wild red deer and fields bounded by beech hedgebanks.

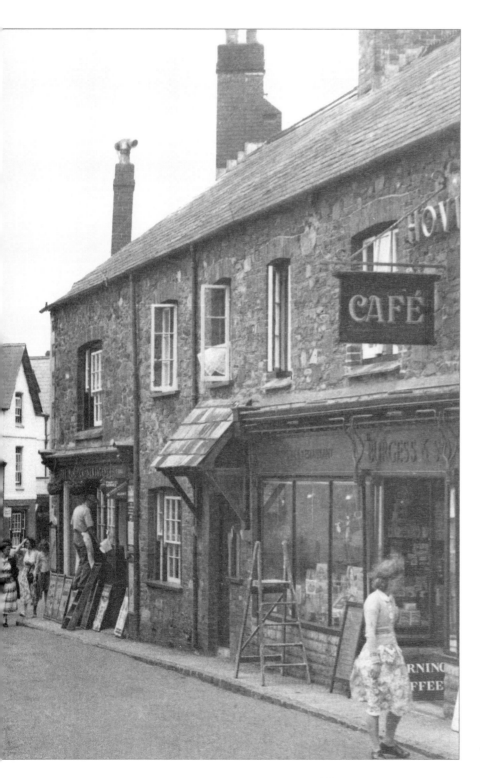

PORLOCK
High Street c1955 P74044

Porlock's High Street has
changed little, and traffic on
the A39 has not increased
enough to initiate a long
proposed by-pass. The café
with the balcony, now the
Countryman Restaurant,
was originally the
Methodist chapel, and
Smith's garage, beyond, is
also a restaurant, taking
trade from passing tourists.

▶ **PORLOCK**
High Street c1960
P74102

This is another scene that has little changed: there is still a chemist's and candy shop on the right and garage on the left, minus petrol pumps. Leach's shops (left) became the library and now three shops. At the end of the street, with the tall chimney, is the 15th-century Doverhay Manor, now Porlock's museum.

◀ **BOSSINGTON**
The Village c1965
B154013

Little has changed here, thanks to the National Trust. Bossington is part of the Holnicote Estate, which was given to the Trust by Sir Francis Acland in 1944. The single-street village is characterised by orchards, walnut trees and cottages with tall chimneys with the backs of bread ovens bulging from their bases.

▲ **ALLERFORD**

The Packhorse Bridge c1955 A34012

This view of Allerford's much photographed 15th-century packhorse bridge and ford looks much the same today. The guesthouse to the right now has a public bar. Beyond rises the side of Selworthy Beacon, forested in the early 19th century by Sir Thomas Acland, owner of the estate.

◄ **SELWORTHY**

The Green c1960 S92020

This scene has looked like this for nearly two centuries. The cottages were built in the 1820s for retired workers on the Acland family's Holnicote Estate. They were medieval farmhouses, remodelled to the fashionable designs of John Nash.

▼ **LUCCOMBE,** *The Village c1955* L355015

Luccombe remains a quiet backwater with traditional thatched and tiled cottages and walks over the surrounding Holnicote Estate. The church of St Mary is a fine example of Perpendicular architecture with beautiful traceried windows.

▲ **SELWORTHY**
Car Park and View c1960 S92023

The car park in front of Selworthy's whitewashed church looks across the Vale of Porlock to the wooded Horner valley and Ley Hill. The scene is much the same today, as the area has been protected by the National Trust since the First World War and as a National Park since 1954.

▶ **WOOTTON COURTENAY**
The Village c1960
W140009

Wootton Courtenay's stores, now a villagers' co-operative, lies opposite the one in this picture - at the end of the middle block on the left. Hidden behind is All Saints' Church with its churchyard cross and huge yew tree. Today this quiet village boasts a vineyard, a restaurant and a water-powered pottery.

MINEHEAD
The 'Bristol Queen'
entering the Harbour
c1960 M84196

Built in 1947, the *Bristol Queen* was considered to be the ultimate in paddle steamer design, and was never to be replaced. She made regular trips up and down the Bristol Channel in the early 1960s, but she was damaged in 1967, and it was considered uneconomical to repair her.

▶ **MINEHEAD**
The Parade c1950 M84101

The Parade was Minehead's market place. The Market Hall with its clock tower is on the right. The World War II air raid shelters had not long been removed from the middle of the street; at the end of the vista the old Plume of Feathers coaching inn was demolished a decade later.

▶ **MINEHEAD**
The Harbour c1950 M84107

Western National service buses (centre) stand on Quay Street - they used to meet steamer passengers. However, most trips from the harbour were pleasure trips, for which the fishing boats had been converted.

▶ **MINEHEAD**
The Avenue c1965
M84250

Originally Station Road, Minehead's Avenue was built in the 1870s to link the newly built railway station with the town centre. Its elegant houses soon became guesthouses, and are now shops. The billboards for the coach offices on the right advertise trips to Exmoor and the Quantocks.

▼ **DUNSTER,** *The Nunnery c1955* D70044

This medieval building is known as The Nunnery, although it never was one; in fact, it was a guesthouse for the nearby priory. Its slate-hung walls are typical of the local style. When this picture was taken it had become dilapidated, and the central cottage was soon afterwards restored by the National Park Authority.

▶ **DUNSTER**
The Yarn Market c1955
D70049

This market, with the medieval Luttrell Arms Hotel to the right and Conygar Tower on the hill behind, has little changed. It was built in 1601 for the sale of the broad and heavy woollen cloths known as Dunsters. It was damaged during a siege of the castle in the Civil War.

◄ DUNSTER
High Street c1955
D70080

Dunster's High Street was built wide to accommodate markets, and at this point it once held a row of shambles, or butcher's shops, in the middle. Dunster Castle, now belonging to the National Trust, was still owned by the Luttrell family at this date; they had occupied it since medieval times.

► CARHAMPTON
The Butchers Arms c1960 C25016

This pub has a date of 1635 in sheep's knucklebones set in the floor of the bar. It was a village meeting place for hundreds of years before the village hall existed, and it is famed for its wassailing ceremony in the orchard behind.

BLUE ANCHOR
The Beach c1955 B124047

Blue Anchor is a hamlet in Carhampton parish, and it takes its name from the local inn. In 1874 it became a halt on the Taunton to Minehead railway line, now the privately run West Somerset Railway. With the railway came tourism, first with beach huts, then chalets, and, in the 1950s, caravan sites.

▼ **OLD CLEEVE,** *The Village c1955* O15004

St Andrew's Church overlooks a row of 17th-century cottages that now have thatched porches. Each has two downstairs rooms divided by a cross passage. Corner Cottage, jutting from the end, is a century older, and has now been refurbished. Beyond is the church schoolroom and the lych gate - from where Monks Path runs to Cleeve Abbey.

► **WATCHET**
The Harbour Entrance c1955 W35063

Watchet long had a busy harbour. In the 19th century, a railway brought Brendon Hills iron ore here for shipment to Wales.
In the 20th century, ships brought in esparto grass for the town's paper mills. The huge tidal range limited the harbour's potential, but now lock gates hold in water for a marina.

◄ KILVE
The Hood Arms
c1965 K22028

Once a haunt of smugglers, this pub became popular with parties, often from afar. Up to a hundred would fill the Club Room for dances and socials. Frank Stevens ran it for many years until 1947, then his wife ran it until 1962. They served cream teas and whortleberry tart on the terrace in summer.

► HOLFORD
Combe House c1955
H93061

This wheel, built in 1820, worked the old tannery, now the Combe House Hotel. It lies at the foot of Holford Glen, the scene of many walks taken by Coleridge and Wordsworth, who lived nearby. The surrounding cottages were built for the tannery workers by the 19th-century owner, James Hayman.

◄ **WHEDDON CROSS**
The Rest and Be Thankful Hotel c1965
W597026

Standing at a crossroads on the ridge between Exmoor and the Brendon Hills, the long haul up the turnpike from Bampton or Minehead gave both the hill and this inn its well-earned name. This early 19th-century inn is used by farmers attending the adjacent Cutcombe Market.

CUTCOMBE
The Village c1965
C739044

The focus of Cutcombe is now Wheddon Cross. Here in the old part of the village were once shops, a school and a pub. A Victorian post box sits in the wall on the right, out of view. The cottages, little changed, carry the names of former occupants: Crockford, Chidgey, Pope, Syms and Miss Bryant.

▲ **EXFORD,** *The Village c1955* E50019

Exford is one of the few Exmoor villages with a green. This scene has little changed, with the Exmoor Stores and the Crown Hotel surviving and still relying on trade from hunting. The kennels of the staghounds are just over the Exe bridge, which is round to the right.

◀ **WINSFORD**
General View c1960
W112018

Here we can see Winsford nestling in the Exe valley below Bye Hill, with the valley of the Winn winding up to the left. The meeting of the rivers with their tiny bridges adds to the charm of the village and its thatched cottages. In the foreground are Closewool sheep, typical of Exmoor.

▼ **WINSFORD,** *The Cross c1960* W112046

Winsford's granite cross commemorates the dead of both World Wars. It is separated from the enclosed village green by the Winn Brook, which is spanned by five little bridges before it reaches the Exe. The village shop, to the left, is still there, and the scene looks much the same today, except that the five conifers are much grown.

▶ **WITHYPOOL**

The Village c1965

W596025

Here Withypool is viewed from its six-arched bridge over the Barle. The squat tower of St Andrew's Church can be seen above the old Methodist chapel (centre). The village shop remains, but the petrol pumps now stand opposite, where ramshackle farm buildings were hidden by trees.

◀ **DULVERTON**
*The View from the
Town Hall Steps
c1960* D60086

This view, little
changed today, looks
up Fore Street to Bank
Square and All Saints'
Church. To the left of
the tower stands the
Belfry Tree, a huge
sycamore which blew
down in a gale a
decade after this
picture was taken.

▶ **DULVERTON**
The Town Hall c1960
D60098

This is Fore Street, which
was built wide to
accommodate fairs and
markets. The 18th-
century Market Hall
became the Town Hall
in 1927, when the steps
were added for access
to the room used for
entertainment and
meetings. The Tantivy
(left) was named after
the coach service that
connected with
Dulverton's railway
station, two miles away.

DULVERTON
*High Street and
The Cottage c1965*
D60102

We are looking towards
Bridge Street and the
River Barle. Across the
river on the hillside is
The Cottage, a mock-
Tudor house with plaster
pargetting standing
amid rhododendrons.
The Lamb Hotel (left),
one of Dulverton's once
numerous pubs, is now
apartments.

DULVERTON, *The Carnarvon Arms Hotel c1960* D60037

This hotel was built in 1873 for the 4th Earl of Carnarvon, who lived at nearby Pixton Park, and it became a centre for
hunting and fishing. It was situated beside Dulverton Station on the Great Western Railway, but the railway closed and the
hotel has become apartments.

SEDGEMOOR

SEDGEMOOR runs from the edge of the Quantocks to the edge of the Mendips. In between lie the Levels, a vast reclaimed marshland. The remains of prehistoric wooden trackways built across the flooded marshes 6000 years ago can still be found here. Today it is mostly pasture divided by rhynes (drainage ditches, pronounced 'reens'), which are lined by pollarded willows. Much of this area lies below the level of high tides in the Bristol Channel, from which the rivers and drains are separated by a low clay ridge and a series of clyses or valve-like sluices. Only the Parrett with its broad, muddy estuary is open to the sea. The river once brought many ships up to Bridgwater, which is now dependent upon the busy M5.

The low ridge of the Polden Hills divides the Levels; the southern part around the Rivers Cary, Tone and Parrett is the traditional Sedgemoor. Somerset people, ever independent, rose behind the Duke of Monmouth in 1685 to oust James II from the throne. Under the Poldens near Westonzoyland they were defeated at the Battle of Sedgemoor, the last battle to be fought on English soil. Many escaping rebels were hunted down, tried by Judge Jeffreys at Taunton and hung from trees.

NETHER STOWEY, *The Village c1955* N8023

This area once held a weekly market. The present tower, built in 1897 for Queen Victoria's Diamond Jubilee, stands on the site of the covered market, which also had a clock tower. The bus shelter to the right of the tower occupies the site of the village gaol.

NETHER STOWEY
Lime Street c1960
N8030

We are looking up Lime Street from its junction with Castle Street; Coleridge's Cottage can be seen at the end on the left. The cottage is now National Trust property; part of it was lived in by Samuel Taylor Coleridge between 1796 and 1800, when he wrote his best known poems, including *Kubla Khan* and *The Ancient Mariner*.

BRIDGWATER, *The Town Bridge c1960* B205084

Spanning the River Parrett, Bridgwater's present Town Bridge was built in 1883, on the site of earlier bridges. Downstream were the docks that at the time handled thousands of ships each year. The river walls have since been raised to prevent flooding.

BRIDGWATER, *The Blake Memorial c1955* B205034

This memorial to Admiral Blake stands in front of the Regency Market House. Erected in 1900, it reads: 'Robert Blake, born in this town 1598, died at sea 1657'. Among his great achievements was his victory at Santa Cruz off Tenerife, where he destroyed a Spanish treasure fleet.

BRIDGWATER
High Street c1950 B205016

Bridgwater prospered in the early 19th century thanks to its brick and tile industry, and many buildings in the High Street date from that time. The reconstruction narrowed the street, which once had a row of shops down the middle. To the left is the spire of St Mary's Church.

▶ **HIGHBRIDGE**
Market Street c1960
H499020

Here on the right is the old town hall, the first offices of Somerset County Council. Demolished in 1984, it once stood opposite the market house, used for the sale of locally made Cheddar and Caerphilly cheese. Outside was a street market selling clothes, furniture and food.

▶ **COSSINGTON**
The Church c1960
C501028

Cossington lies on the Polden Hills, overlooking the Levels. Cottages are grouped around the church and the manor (right), an early 19th-century building with bargeboards carved like lace. The earlier manor house belonged to the Brent family, who are commemorated in the church.

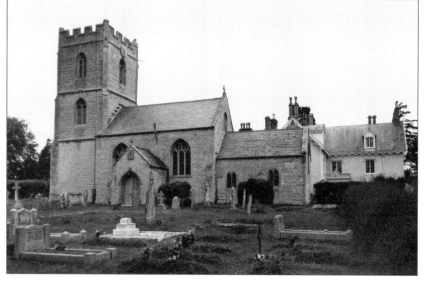

▶ **PURITON**
Middle Street c1955
P384005

Puriton's brick and tile industry has now gone, but Middle Street is much the same today. Biggs' general store (right), now the post office, sits here above Good's Farm. To the left is the grey lias wall of Admiral Blake's home, Puriton Manor. The original house does not survive, but the great arched gateway does.

▲ **BASON BRIDGE,** *The Brue River and Merry Lane c1960* B869318

Merry Lane runs for a mile along the Brue from Bason Bridge to Cripp's Farm, providing easy access for fishermen. There is good coarse fishing here, and the area around the old dairy factory is noted for its carp. Club competitions are held, except during the close season in spring months.

◄ **BASON BRIDGE**
*The Station and the
River Brue c1955*
B869005

Bason Bridge is part of East Huntspill village. Here a railway ran alongside the Brue from Highbridge to Glastonbury. The line served the Wiltshire United Dairies factory that opened in 1909 - it was later taken over by Unigate. The line closed in 1984.

▲ **HUNTSPILL,** *High Road c1960* H510005

West Huntspill, which we see here, grew from a conglomeration of agricultural hamlets straggling across the Levels. The Globe Hotel (right) is now much extended, and has been renamed the Scarlet Pimpernel. The Victorian Methodist church beyond and Georgian Ilex Court beyond that remain, backed by orchards and separated by closes of new houses.

◀ **WEDMORE**
Church Street c1955
W169026

We are looking up Wedmore's Church Street, past St Mary Magdalene's Church; we can just see the Old Vicarage in the distance. On fair days, sheep and pigs were penned outside the George Inn, and hooks to hold the hurdling can still be found on its walls. Gypsies also sold horses here, and there was much drunkenness.

BURNHAM-ON-SEA, *High Street c1965* B249210

Once known as Alfred Street, Burnham's main shopping street was an avenue at one time; but the trees were removed to accommodate traffic. It runs parallel with the Esplanade, and holidaymakers swell the numbers of shoppers in the summer.

◀ **EAST BRENT**

The War Memorial c1965 E61014

East Brent's green is surrounded by white- and cream-washed cottages. Here its Anglican and Wesleyan churches each provided schools. In a corner of the green the recently restored war memorial has life-sized statues of First World War servicemen.

▼ **EAST BRENT**

The Shops c1965 E61016

We are looking along a rhyne, or ditch, across the Levels; little has changed here today. The Brent Knoll Inn, named after the 500ft hill that it faces, is still there. The shop on the Old Bristol Road to the right is now a wholesale ice cream and frozen food supplier's.

AXBRIDGE
King John's Hunting Lodge c1955 A254062

The Lodge, a house dating from about 1500, belongs to the National Trust and houses Axbridge Museum. It takes its name from a carved king's head on the corner, the sign of the King's Head Inn. It is reputed to be a likeness of King John, who hunted in nearby Mendip forest.

CHEDDAR, *The Gorge c1955* C71139

Cheddar Gorge is dry, but here at the end of the village the River Yeo emerges from its subterranean course. It was dammed into ponds to feed corn and paper mills, with sluices (foreground) to remove trapped silt. To the right is the entrance to Jacob's Ladder - 274 steps leading to an observation tower.

TAUNTON DEANE

THE VALE of Taunton Deane is a fertile plain, with tongue-like valleys running between the Quantock, Brendon and Blackdown Hills. Its small, lush fields divided by hedgebanks were famed for orchards and cider. To the east of Taunton lie the Somerset moors, an area of wet, acidic soils. The Isle of Athelney stood out from the marshland - here in AD878 Alfred, the young King of Wessex, took refuge from Danish invaders and reputedly burnt the cakes. The Anglo-Saxon Chronicle records that he then went to Selwood to raise all the people of Somerset, 'Sumorsaete ealle', to rise against the invaders, who were subsequently defeated; the phrase became the county motto.

Wellington is overlooked by the Wellington Monument, standing on the escarpment of the Blackdown Hills. The Duke of Wellington chose to take his name from the town, and he was given the lands of its manor in thanks for his military victories. Nearby, the county town of Taunton retains little of its local character; but it has the remains of a castle, and the tower of St Mary's Church is the most magnificent of the Somerset type.

WIVELISCOMBE, *High Street c1955* W315015

Wivey's main street was by-passed in 1980. The Lion, the town's main hotel, became a church, and Baigent's the draper's next door a restaurant. The building by the pole on the left was built as a Public Dispensary in 1804, and provided free medical attention for the poor.

49

▶ **WIVELISCOMBE**
The Square c1960
W315026

The tile-hung building to the right of the Square has woodwork elaborately carved with figures, fruit and mythical animals. Constructed as the Court House in 1881, it became a bank, then the library. The tall building opposite was the Town Hall, which had lost its colonnaded front when it became a shop.

◀ **BISHOP'S LYDEARD**
West Street c1955
B868007

The building on the right of this picture was built as the village police station in 1915, and contained a cell. The beautiful 15th-century tower of the church of St Mary the Virgin, beyond, is of the Somerset type, and stands over a hundred feet high.

▲ **WELLINGTON,** *High Street c1955* W45034

Showing one of its clock faces, Wellington's Market and Town Hall was built in 1831 on property belonging to the Duke of Wellington. It was redeveloped in 1885, when the old Market House Inn to its left became the post office, and again in 1937.

◄ **WELLINGTON**
High Street c1960
W45078

Wellington's East Street was widened to become the High Street in the 19th century. The ornate, ballustraded Tone Libraries shop on the right was built onto the front of the old Swan Inn in 1907, and the Town Mills continued operating in the street until 1969.

▲ **TAUNTON**
Fore Street c1955 T16060

Taunton's Market House, now mainly
offices, stands on the site of the former
covered market. Open markets are
occasionally still held on the far side of
the building, where the Memorial Cross
has now been moved. Known as the
Burmese War Memorial, it commemorates
19th-century battles fought by the
Somerset Regiment, whose barracks
were nearby.

▶ **TAUNTON**
Fore Street c1955 (Detail) T16060

TAUNTON
*Corporation Street
and County Hall c1960*
T16074

Somerset's County Hall was transferred here from Weston-super-Mare in 1935. The new building was beautifully designed by Vincent Harris, and it is situated next to the municipal offices at Shire Hall. Corporation Street linked this with the former municipal buildings in the town centre, hence the name.

NORTH CURRY, *Jubilee Square c1960* N219019

Viewed from the post office, this memorial to Queen Victoria is known as the Pepperpot because of its shape. Five roads meet at the square, including Church Road, which contains with many beautiful listed cottages. The centre of the village is used to hold the annual May Fair.

EAST LYNG
The Village c1955
E239012

Known just as Lyng, East Lyng is strung out along the busy road over the Levels from Taunton to Street. The Rose and Crown (centre left) survives. The tall yew trees, now gone, were already old when this picture was taken, but they gave their name to adjacent Yew Tree House.

EAST LYNG, *St Bartholomew's Church c1955* E239016

St Bartholomew's Church has a beautiful Somerset tower. Monks from the former abbey at nearby Athelney are reputed to have built part of the church and carved its bench ends with figures, some of which are depicted jumping over rhynes. Its graveyard spills across the road to the village hall. The garage and old farmhouse next to it remain.

SOUTH SOMERSET

THE RIVERS Parrett, Yeo and Isle carry tongues of the Levels into the southern parts of the county. Here an arc of rolling vales and scarps runs from the Wiltshire Downs to the wooded Blackdown Hills. It is a geologically varied area where chalks, limestones and clays suit arable farming. From Ilminster to Ilchester huge cornfields cover medieval open fields separated by low banks. Farms still cluster in the villages, which retain much of their ancient character.

Many southern hills are capped by Iron Age forts, such as the one at South Cadbury, reputed to have been King Arthur's Camelot. The fort at Ham Hill overlooks the quarries for the streaky, honey-coloured limestone that characterises the district's beautiful country houses and estate villages. Under the hill lies Montacute House, built for Elizabethan judge Sir Edward Phelips, whilst a few miles to the south west the Earls Poulett much altered their imposing mansion at Hinton St George. Their village retains some of the county's finest Tudor and Stuart vernacular architecture.

BUCKLAND ST MARY, *The Post office and the Church c1960* B841014

In the mid 19th century the wealthy Rev John Lance built himself a large vicarage and replaced the small 15th-century church with one so large that it was nicknamed the 'Cathedral of the Blackdown Hills'. Along with a post office there were a grocery, a butcher's, a cobbler's, a tailor's and a baker's in the village at this time.

▶ COMBE ST NICHOLAS
Combe Head c1960
C737042

This thatched cottage, now slated, was a 17th-century farmhouse, then two cottages; now it is the lodge for Combe Head House. Inside the house gates (left) are the graves of two pugs, inscribed 'always on guard'. In 1960 the lodge still had a garden privy and was inhabited by a family with nine children.

◀ **CHARD**
Fore Street c1955
C58028

Chard High Street's pavements were built wide to hold market stalls. The clock tower on the left was added to the Town Hall in 1834. The refurbished building was formerly the Corn Exchange, then the Guildhall. The Ball Inn to its left, once thatched, has been demolished to make way for a Woolworth's.

▲ **BROADWAY,** *The Village c1965* B867008

Pretty cottages still line Broadway Road. Some were used for the cottage industry of glove making, but most were farmhouses, and the village is still an agricultural settlement with a working farm at its centre. In the street are the Bell Inn and 16th-century almshouses.

▶ **CHARD**
Fore Street c1955
C58032

Seen from Lower High Street, this was the main A30 through the town and a busy stop for buses and coaches. Halfway down the left of the street, the whitewashed George Hotel, now renamed, developed as a coaching inn. The spire behind is that of Chard's large Congregational church.

▼ **ILMINSTER,** *The Crown Hotel and the Triangle c1950* 17005

The Ilminster by-pass now takes traffic from this street, and little has changed here. The shop and garage on the left are now houses, and new houses stand high on Strawberry Bank beyond. To the right, there is still a fish and chip shop by West Street, which runs down to the Minster.

► **ILMINSTER**
The Market Place c1955
17013

We are looking across the Square to East Street. The colonnaded Market Hall, rebuilt in 1813, dominates the centre of Ilminster. The tall building to the left is the post office. Originally a warehouse built after a fire in 1915, it is made of locally produced blocks of crushed Ham Stone concrete.

◄ WINSHAM
Church Street c1955
W575021

Originally the site of the village pump, this cross is at the junction of five roads. The George Inn, behind the cross, and the King's Arms (left) are now just houses. The post office/shop by the Morris is still there, along with the Jubilee Hall, opposite, which was built for meetings.

► CREWKERNE
St Bartholemew's Church c1960
C185050

The size of Crewkerne's parish church reflects the town's former prosperity. On one side its huge windows leave room for little more than buttresses between. Its west front is like that of Bath Abbey, flanked by gargoyled turrets. Amongst the many other carvings is a church orchestra in the south porch.

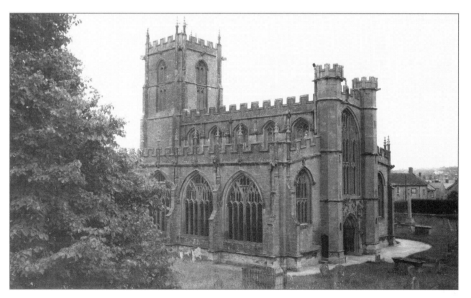

◄ **MERRIOTT**
Lower Street c1955
M370007

Lower Street is the part of the square of Merriott's main streets nearest the Parrett. It has many old Ham stone cottages, some thatched, and some with stone mullioned windows. To the right of the lorry are the Swan Inn and Manor Farmhouse and Manor Cottage, dated 1663 and haunted by a coach and horses.

◀ **HINTON ST GEORGE**
The Cross c1960
H513019

Viewed shortly after its restoration, this cross with a shaft and a figure of St John the Baptist dates from the 15th century - the ball on top dates from the time of Queen Anne. Nearby is Priory Farm, the remains of a 12th-century priory, and the George and Crown Inn, where Fair Day parades culminated.

▲ **SEAVINGTON ST MICHAEL,** *The Village c1955* S792001

The A303 now bypasses this agricultural settlement with its tiny church. Old cottages have stone-framed windows and doorways, and new houses blend in colour with their crushed Ham stone concrete. This scene is little changed: the Volunteer Inn, minus whitewash, survives along with the phone box; behind it is the Old Post Office.

◀ **SHEPTON BEAUCHAMP**
The Village c1955
S787008

We are looking down North Street from the Duke of York pub, and this scene looks much the same today. The 'Family Shop' - the post office and stores on the left - is now a watch repairer's. The baker's next door still has its Hovis sign, but it is a computer business now.

▼ **SOUTH PETHERTON,** *Monks Corner c1960* S412004

This war memorial, built in 1921, stands in the corner of the parish churchyard. Across the road is Monks Corner, a reminder that the church once belonged to the priory at Bruton. Adjoining this is Crown Lane, named after the Crown Inn, which was demolished in 1984. Its old fives wall (fives is a ball game played in a walled court) was saved and restored.

▶ **FIVEHEAD**
The Parish Church c1960
F228005

Fivehead lies on a ridge overlooking the Levels. St Martin's Church dates from the 13th century, but it had a major Victorian overhaul. Despite this, the tower had to be rebuilt when it fell apart in the early 20th century. The Village Hall with its bell tower (left) was the village school from 1874 to 1971.

◄ CURRY RIVEL
Fore Street c1960
C734018

Curry Rivel's High Street, still with many shops, is strung along the A378. Behind Jackson's the ironmonger's (left) was once Bernard's the baker's, now a private house. The house before the Bell Inn, at the end of the street, is now a garage.

► DRAYTON
The Village and the War Memorial c1955
D254003

Drayton's thatched, grey lias war memorial stands across Church Street from the Drayton Arms. Behind stands Church House, once a meeting-place for monks from nearby Muchelney Abbey. Behind that, St Catherine's Church is nearly hidden by two huge and ancient yews, which flank a 15th-century cross.

LANGPORT
*The Hanging Chapel
and Old School House
c1960* L365047

The Hanging Chapel is
above the archway to the
left, hidden behind the
trees. It was the town's
guild or corporation
chapel. To the right
stands the 19th-century
Old School House, no
longer thatched.

HUISH EPISCOPI, *The View from All Saints' Church c1965* H527071

Huish Episcopi extends around Langport on the Levels. Its church of St Mary was rebuilt after a fire in the 15th century, and the scorching can still be seen around the Norman doorway. Its beautiful pinnacled tower is seen here from the contemporaneous tower of All Saints' Church in Langport.

MARTOCK, *The Pinnacle and the Market House c1955* M42015

Built in the 1750s, Martock's Market House originally held a row of shambles or butchers' shops. It became a fire station, the council house and an ex-servicemen's club before restoration in 1954 for council meetings. The original Pinnacle, a copy of a column at Wilton House, was destroyed by a lorry and replaced.

STOKE SUB HAMDON, *High Street c1960* S261029

This village prospered thanks to the quarries on Ham Hill, and the High Street has some fine 17th-century houses built in Ham stone. A glove-making industry grew in the 19th century, when the street housed members of the Southcombe family, factory owners. The once numerous shops have become reduced to a handful.

MONTACUTE
The Church c1960
M92020

St Catherine's Church is part Norman, and contains monuments to the Phelips family dating from the 15th century. The 16th-century tower has a unique 300-year-old clock. A descendant of the maker wound it daily for 65 years, only retiring in 1984, since when it has been restored.

YEOVIL, *Princes Street c1950* Y11017

This wide street once held a cattle market. It now has one-way traffic, but little has changed here except that building societies and estate agents have taken over the shops. Genge's & Austin's department store (left), now closed, gave its name to 'Genge's Corner'.

YEOVIL

Middle Street c1955 Y11057

This street, now pedestrianised, was a busy part of the A30 trunk road. It was widened a century ago to cope with the increasing traffic. We are looking down from the Triangle, and we can see the Freeman, Hardy & Willis shoe shop on the left, AJ Perham's Hair Cutting Rooms on the right, and the South Western Gas Board at the end of the street.

▶ **MUDFORD**
Main Street c1960
M383006

This photograph looks from the Old School down the A359 to the bridge over the Yeo, where a muddy ford once gave the village its name; this scene has little changed. To the right, hidden behind its former skittle alley, is the Half Moon Inn, which once belonged to the local Brutton's brewery.

▲ **SOMERTON,** *The Cross c1960* S147022

Somerton's Market or Butter Cross is dated 1673. It adjoins the Town Hall, which is also 17th-century. The building behind the Jaguar was built in 1550; now the Market House Café, it has been used as tea rooms for many years.

◀ **ILCHESTER**

The Cross Roads c1965
I75021

Ilchester's triangular 'village green' is faced by Georgian houses and the Town Hall. The Ham stone market cross, now restored, was erected in 1795. In the distance is the church of St Mary Major with its massive 13th-century tower, square at the base and octagonal at the top.

◄ **KEINTON MANDEVILLE**
The Cross-Roads c1955
K180004

We are looking down the High Street from Castle Street, where Victorian actor Sir Henry Irving was born. There were building stone quarries around the village - the Quarry Inn is lower down the street, and the gardens are separated by upright slabs of lias. The shop on the right is now offices.

◀ **SOMERTON**
*Broad Street
c1960* S147067

Somerton was once a thriving medieval town with fairs, markets, trade and inns. Cattle were sold at the Rother Beast Market in Broad Street, which had standings with gutters down each side, hence the width of the street.

▲ **SPARKFORD,** *The Sparkford Inn c1955* S788005

Now by-passed, Sparkford grew as a service area on the A303 and the railway. The inn, dating from the 15th century, was a posting house; the old stables have been converted to garages. The inn incorporates the Agricultural Hall that was used for farmers' meetings and hunt balls.

◀ **CASTLE CARY**
The Horse Pond c1955
C611005

This pond is a remnant of the castle moat, which was reshaped in 1784. It was home to a pair of swans for years until it was deemed unsuitable, and for the Millennium a swan statue was erected in the water near the war memorial.

▼ **CASTLE CARY,** *Fore Street c1965* C611056

The White Hart here has a long history. Fore Street once had many thatched cottages and a stream running down one side, but it was rebuilt in the 19th century, when the town prospered with the woollen industry. That industry was replaced by shoe making until the 1960s.

▶ **CASTLE CARY**
The Roundhouse c1965
C611057

Also known as the Blind House from its lack of windows, the Roundhouse was the village lock-up. Built in 1779, it sometimes held children playing truant from school. Markets and fairs were held here - the Market House is out of view to the right.

◄ BRUTON
High Street c1965
B842037

Bruton's High Street prospered from medieval times with the woollen industry, which grew along the Brue - gardens behind the houses ran down to the river. Silk mills later developed at the bottom of the street. In this street are Sexey's almshouses, dating from 1638.

► WINCANTON
Market Place c1960
W599069

Here, behind the one way sign we can see the Town Hall. Used mainly for entertainment, it was erected over the market house in 1769, but it has since been rebuilt. The library has now moved, along with the Court House, which was once above it.

WINCANTON
Market Place c1965
W599101

Wincanton's High Street was part of the main route between London and the west. The Bear Hotel (right) was a coaching inn; the present building dates from the 18th century. The adjoining Smith's Library has long been a stationer's shop - it originally belonged to the local historian George Sweetman.

CUCKLINGTON, *St Lawrence's Church c1965* C740095

St Lawrence's Church provides good views towards Wincanton and the hills on the boundary with Dorset. Its tower has a cupola and plaque dating from the restoration after a storm in 1703. Inside is a chapel to St Barbara with a 15th-century picture of her in stained glass.

MENDIP

THE MENDIPS form a bleak upland amongst a rich tapestry of valleys and ancient villages. The plateau with its dry limestone walls is bare and largely uninhabited except for the lead mining village of Priddy. From the top virtually the whole county can be seen on a clear day. Axbridge, with its medieval square, and Cheddar, famed for its cheese and gorge, are geographically in Mendip and politically in Sedgemoor. A string of villages follows the springs running from under the limestone. To the east lies Shepton Mallet, a typical Somerset wool town with many buildings of the grey limestone from the neighbouring village of Doulting.

2200 years ago, people were living in houses built on stilts in lakes around Glastonbury. Three Saxon kings were buried at Glastonbury Abbey, reputedly founded by Joseph of Arimathea and the resting place of King Arthur and Guinevere. The medieval abbey led the way in draining the Levels, growing apples and grapes, keeping sheep and founding the county's woollen industry, which funded many fine churches. In AD909 Wells' church became a cathedral, making the town England's smallest city.

LOWER WEARE, *The Main Road c1955* L546010

Before the construction of the M5 in the 1970s, the A38 was busy with West Country traffic. Under the Mendips, the Old Post House (by the phone box) and Weare House (to its left), now private houses, and the Lamb Inn (behind the photographer) offered refreshment and accommodation to travellers.

▲ **WESTBURY-SUB-MENDIP**
The Post Office c1955 W598002

Village stocks were once attached to this cross, which stands at the junction of roads to Wells, Draycot and Westbury. Its six octagonal tiers of steps date from the 15th century, but the shaft is more recent. The post office/stores is now a computer business, with a new stores opposite.

▶ **GLASTONBURY**
The Cross c1955 G12029

Viewed from North Load Street, Glastonbury's Market Cross was built in 1846 on the site of a medieval covered cross and fountain. The Abbey Gate Restaurant to the right is not 14th-century as it claims, but the adjacent Abbey Gate is.

GLASTONBURY
The Tor c1965 G12078

Glastonbury Tor once stood like an island in the surrounding marshes, and it has been linked with King Arthur's Avalon. The 13th-century tower on top of this famous landmark is all that remains of St Michael's Church.

WELLS, *The Market Place c1960* W47052

Wells Cathedral is reached through the 15th-century Penniless Porch (centre left), so named because beggars sheltered there. The gateway to the right is part of the 19th-century Market House, which became the post office. The fountain dates from the 18th century, and water flows down a channel made in 1803 'for cleansing and fire fighting'.

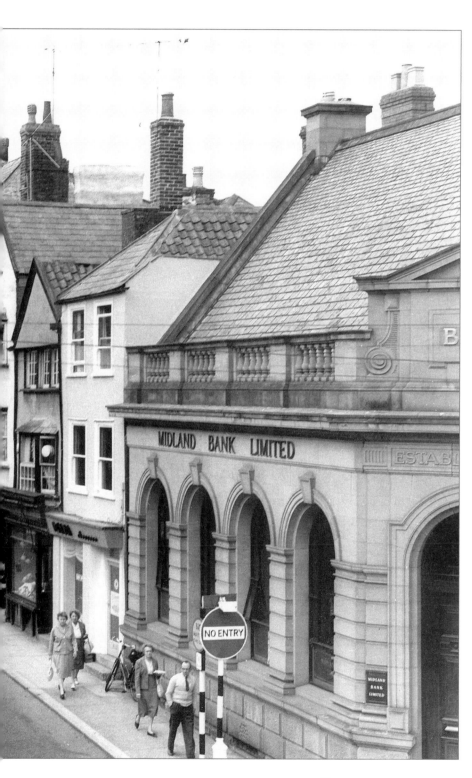

WELLS
Sadler Street c1960
W47065

Much of Sadler Street developed in the 14th century. At the bottom right is Dean's Eye, a gateway built in 1453. The Old Priory Café (left) is a jettied medieval building with a pargetted (carved plaster) 17th-century façade. The street was subject to an enhancement scheme in 2001.

◄ **PILTON**
The Post Office c1960
P383016

Pilton is famed for its pop festivals, which started in 1970. Its crossroads was known as Conduit Square because of an underground drainage system. The store was originally the White Hart Hotel, with a brewery behind, and the Crown Inn to its right was the tap room for the coachmen. The post office was opposite.

◄ DINDER
High Street c1965
D249008

Along Dinder's main street the Doulting Water was diverted to provide running water for the inhabitants. Overlooking the water is a row of 16th-century gabled and mullioned cottages, two farmhouses, a Victorian school and a former forge and pub that still shows the sign of the Dragon on the Wheel, a local family crest.

▲ **DITCHEAT,** *The Village c1955* D255002

The name of this village derives from 'dyke gate', referring to the control of water through sluices. The Manor House (left), formerly Ditcheat House, was built for Robert Hopton early in the 17th century. One of its stone mullioned windows has a pane painted with the arms of the Dawe family, the manor's later owners.

◄ SHEPTON MALLET
High Street c1955
S111021

A Showerings van and shop can be seen here on the right. This local family made cider and beer and delivered it door to door. Promotion of their Babycham perry in the 1950s made the four Showering brothers wealthy. In a 1970s redevelopment, car parks were built behind the shops, and the street was pedestrianised.

▲ **SHEPTON MALLET,** *The Square and the Cross c1965* S111023

This cross was built in the 13th-century market place in around 1500, and was used for the sale of butter, eggs and chickens. Adjacent were 'shambles' or stalls - the base of one still remains. Outside the Bell Inn was a stage for preaching on market days.

◀**LITTON**
General View c1960
L547011

Litton has long been an agricultural settlement, with surrounding hillsides terraced by lynchets from medieval ploughing. The stream running through the village was dammed in the 19th century to supply water for Bristol and three local mills. The church has many ancient features, including carved heads outside and benches and a pulpit inside.

▲ **MIDSOMER NORTON**
The War Memorial and the River Somer c1965 M125017

Here the River Somer runs along the middle of the High Street, flowing over small weirs known as 'flashes'. It emerges from under the Island in the Square and runs down to Radstock. A tunnel now diverts its once frequent floods.

◄ **STRATTON-ON-THE-FOSSE**
The Memorial c1955 S790014

Stratton is strung along the Fosse Way, a Roman road. Its elaborate and recently restored war memorial stands on the junction with Church Lane. The main feature of the village, once dependant upon coal mining, is now Downside Abbey and School.

► **HOLCOMBE**
The Post Office
c1960 H92018

In medieval times Holcombe was built up a hill to escape the plague in the old village below. It prospered thanks to coal mining, and packhorses carried the coal down the street to the Fosse Way. Nowadays it is a prosperous commuting area, and modern semis punctuate the old stone cottages.

◄**KILMERSDON**
The Village c1955
K181019

The 100ft tower of St Peter and St Paul's Church dominates this estate village of grey lias cottages. The tower is in the Somerset style, and is decorated with fifty carved figures. Below, the Regency Joliffe Arms looks across to the village lock-up, now a bus shelter.

▲ **MELLS,** *Gay Street c1950* M56019

The grocery shop here on the left, popular for children's sweets, was run until 1952 by Misses Gambol and 'Sniffy' Baker. They touted ice creams around the village to the call of 'I scream, you scream, we scream for ice cream'. Audrey Axford then ran it until its closure in 1965.

◄**MELLS**
The Green c1965 M56038

Mells was the village of fabled Jack Horner, who misappropriated its deeds when the landowning monastery was dissolved. The village grew with coal, quarrying, an iron works and cloth making. The green lies on its western edge, with a school, farm and cottages that now support businesses such as internet working and orchid growing.

FROME
The Market Place
c1950 F58005

A market has been held here since 1086. Boyle Cross was a fountain erected in 1871 and used for washing fish for the market. On the right is Lloyd's Bank, and beyond it is the entrance to Cheap Street. The road below was frequently flooded by the River Frome.

FROME, *Cheap Street c1950* F58007

Frome grew with the cloth industry in medieval times. Although the industry declined in the 18th century, from which time many of the buildings did not alter, the last mill did not close until the 1960s. The houses lining Cheap Street date mainly from the 17th century, but some are earlier.

FROME, *Cheap Street c1965* F58067

This street's name comes from the Anglo-Saxon 'cepin', meaning a 'place of trade', and here its shops include opticians, tobacconists, dry cleaners, book and toy shops and the Crusty Loaf bakers with its loaf sign. The central stream maintains the medieval character whilst the arched lamp holder was one of several erected in the 1890s.

STOKE ST MICHAEL
The Square c1955
S789005

Straggling along Oakhill Road, Stoke St Michael is now subject to traffic from surrounding quarries. The post office and stores survives. Nearby is the 17th-century Knatchbull Arms, and just below the Square is a new footbridge and streamside walks to caves.

BECKINGTON, *Bath Road c1955* B402011

Bath Road is an extension of the village, which grew with the wool trade in the 17th and 18th centuries. Until a by-pass came in 1990, it carried both the A36 and A361. In 1927 a recreation ground was built at the end of the road to keep children from the heavy traffic.

NORTON ST PHILIP, *From the Church Tower c1960* N218011

The 70ft tower of the church of St Philip and St James appears to be made of pieces from another building. Below is the Gothic-style village school, built in 1827. The 17th-century gable-fronted cottage on the right is one of several Cotswold-style cottages in the village.

NORTH SOMERSET

THE FAILAND HILLS and outlying ridges of the Mendips divide the North Somerset Levels. The popular tourist and commuter town of Weston-super-Mare is spread along the reclaimed land backing Weston Bay between wooded Worlebury Hill and the estuary of the River Axe. It is now spreading northwards to the estuary of the Yeo, which once carried barges to the foot of the Mendips at Congresbury. The Bristol Channel proper begins at Weston, and Clevedon and Portishead lie beside the muddy waters of the Severn Estuary. They have also become commuter towns for Bristol, although Portishead has its docks and industry.

WESTON-SUPER-MARE
Central Promenade 1950 W69068

We are looking over Weston Bay and the sands from near the Grand Pier; beyond we can see (from left to right) Knightstone Harbour, Glentworth Bay and Birnbeck and Knightstone Roads, with the spire of Holy Trinity Church beyond. Buses replaced the trams, which ran until 1937.

WESTON-SUPER-MARE
The Grand Pier c1955
W69079

This pier was built in 1904, and the pavilion at the end was rebuilt after a fire in 1930. This was used as a theatre for shows, dances and amusements. By the 1950s bingo had become popular, and the walkway down the pier was covered.

▼ **CONGRESBURY,** *The Cross c1960* C234014

This 15th-century cross lies at a crossroads on the Bristol to Weston-super-Mare road; the adjacent Ship and Castle was a coaching inn. Its lower steps have been buried by the raising of the road. Fairs were once held here, and coal barges tied up at wharves nearby.

► **CLEVEDON**

The Pier and the Royal Pier Hotel c1965 C116048

This pier and hotel were both built in 1869. By the 1950s the pier was making a loss, although it remained popular. Lack of maintenance led to its collapse in 1970. A preservation trust was set up, taking many years to raise the money for restoration.

◀ **CLEVEDON**
The Triangle c1955
C116056

This was the original village, and it became the hub of Clevedon when the railway station was built there in 1847. The clock tower was built by the potter Sir Edmund Elton for Queen Victoria's Diamond Jubilee in 1897, by which time the shops were spreading towards the sea front with tourist development.

▶ **PORTISHEAD**
The Boating Lake c1960 P90090

Portishead's Marine Lake lies in the recreation ground behind the Esplanade running along Woodhill Bay. A swannery lay on the wooded islet in the pear-shaped lake, and a paddling pool was added later. The extensive dockland area lay out of sight behind the wooded hill and the power station.

PILL, *The Ferry c1960* P141011

The ferry ran from Crockerne Pill to Shirehampton, seen here across the Avon. It closed in 1974 with the opening of the M5 bridge, which carried a walkway and cycle track along with the motorway. Little commercial traffic now passes through to Bristol. Gone too are the once numerous pilot boats and boat yards.

BRISTOL

LONG a county in its own right, Bristol has never strictly been part of Somerset. From Domesday times it grew as a trading centre, and temporarily became England's second city. In medieval times the course of the River Frome was altered to make a deep water dock, and in the early 19th century a huge floating harbour created a constant water level for the city centre docks. The Industrial Revolution, which made its mark on the city through railways and shipbuilding, also took trade elsewhere. In 1877 docks were opened at Avonmouth and Portishead and in 1977 at Portbury, taking trade and industry out of the city. Today, the old docks have become a popular recreation area. The city still prospers and spreads as a centre for communications and high technology industries.

BRISTOL, *The Centre c1950* B212265

Here is a view over Colston Avenue to Colston Street, with Colston Hall theatre just hidden behind the General Insurance building (centre right). All were named after Edward Colston, a 17th- and 18th-century local philanthropist. The half-timbered building to the left is the bus and coach office. The Bristol Commercial Vehicle Company it advertises made buses locally.

BRISTOL
The Centre 1953
B212283

Here a crown in the flowerbeds in Colston Avenue marks the Queen's coronation. The church tower is that of St John the Baptist, which stands over one of the medieval gateways into the city. The centre was heavily bombed during World War II, and a new shopping area was built at Broadmead, beyond the tower.

CLIFTON
*The Suspension Bridge
c1950* C120189

Clifton grew as a resort in the 18th century. A competition to design its bridge was won by I K Brunel; work began in 1831, but the funds ran out, and it was not completed until 1864, after Brunel's death. At 245ft above the Avon gorge, it has attracted many suicides and, lately, bungee jumpers.

SHIREHAMPTON, *Avonmouth from Penpole Point c1950* S270016

20th-century estates have all but joined Shirehampton to Bristol and Avonmouth. The original 18th-century nucleus around the High Street and the church was still enclosed by orchards and elms in 1950, and Georgian houses still overlook a green.

BATH AND NORTH-EAST SOMERSET

THIS NORTH-EASTERN corner of the county incorporates parts of both the Mendips and the Cotswolds, divided by the River Avon. Along the river the suburbs of Bristol have reached out to engulf villages and towns such as Keynsham. To the west, particularly around the valley of the River Chew and its lake, the area has a rural charm belying its industrial heritage: the area once boasted many water-powered mills manufacturing copper, brass and leather goods. To the east were hundreds of coal mines, and the valleys were criss-crossed with railways and canals. Spoil heaps have rapidly grown over, and it is difficult to believe that the last mine closed as recently as 1973.

Lead mines were worked from as early as AD 49, and around that time the hot mineral springs at Bath attracted the Romans for relaxation. Their Fosse Way ran through Bath on its way from Exeter to Lincoln in a straight line, to be followed by modern roads. The remains of the Roman baths attracted Stuart royalty, and by Hanoverian times Bath had become fashionable. Beau Nash encouraged high society, and the quarry owner Ralph Allen and the architect John Wood created a city unequalled for its Georgian buildings.

WEST HARPTREE, *The Square c1955* W1813128

Once known for its mines and caves, West Harptree sits between the Mendip ridge and Chew Valley Lake. The Crown Inn (left) survives, along with the village shop on the right and the adjacent little shop, now a beauty salon. Out of the picture to the right is the Old School, dated 1852.

▶ **WEST HARPTREE**
The Village c1960
W181001

Here the village is seen from the churchyard, which adjoins a beautiful Jacobean manor house. The triangle with the phone box was once a grassy area where there were hustings at election times. The signpost now sits in a flowerbed, and there is a new phone box next to the Crown Inn.

◀ **BISHOP SUTTON**
Chew Valley Lake c1960 B310017

Coal was produced from several mines around Bishop Sutton until 1929. There was also a large flour mill here; but now the village relies on recreation from the 1,200 acre Chew Valley Lake lying to its west. The lake was built in the 1950s to supply water for Bristol.

▶ **KEYNSHAM**
The Church and Station Road c1955 K64025

St John's Church stands at the busy crossroads of the High Street and Station Road, which runs towards Fry's (now Cadbury's) chocolate factory at Somerdale. Overspill from Bristol more than quadrupled the town's population in the 1950s. The ornate lamp standard survived several knocks before a 1960s by-pass relieved the congestion.

◀ **SALTFORD**
The Village c1955 S839004

Saltford's original village lies on a hillside tunnelled underneath by the Great Western Railway. The village grew thanks to railway workers and commuters, and shops moved onto the ribbon development on the Bristol to Bath road - we can see a post office, an optician's, a chemist's, a Co-op and a petrol station.

BATH
Milsom Street c1965
B33038

This famous shopping
street started in the 1760s
as a row of elegant houses
designed by the architect
John Wood. Down the street
on the left is the Octagon:
originally a Georgian
chapel, it was restored in
1951 as an exhibition centre
and is now a photography
gallery.

▶ **BATH**
*North Parade and
the Abbey 1949*
B33104

The architect John Wood the Elder planned the Parades as part of an area based on the architecture of ancient Rome. Terrace Walk, with the abbey behind, ran between the 18th-century Harrison's and Lindsay's Assembly rooms, and the wide pavements were for promenading.

◀ **BATH**
*York Street and the
Roman Baths c1955*
B33099

This area was part of a reconstruction scheme in the 1790s. The statues of Romans and the balustrade to the right were added in 1897, along with a colonnade around the Roman baths below.

▲ **COMBE DOWN,** *Church Road c1965* C143051

Now part of the City of Bath, this once provided access to the Bath stone quarries of the 18th-century magnate Ralph Allen. Westbury Avenue, to the right, was named because of its view to Westbury White Horse in Wiltshire. The Little Shop was formerly a stationer's, and Sanders, to its right, was the post office.

◄ **SWAINSWICK**
The Church c1965 S272011

The church of St Mary the Virgin at Upper Swainswick dates from Norman times. To the right of the porch is a pretty decorated window dating from around 1300, and beyond lie the buildings of Manor Farm.

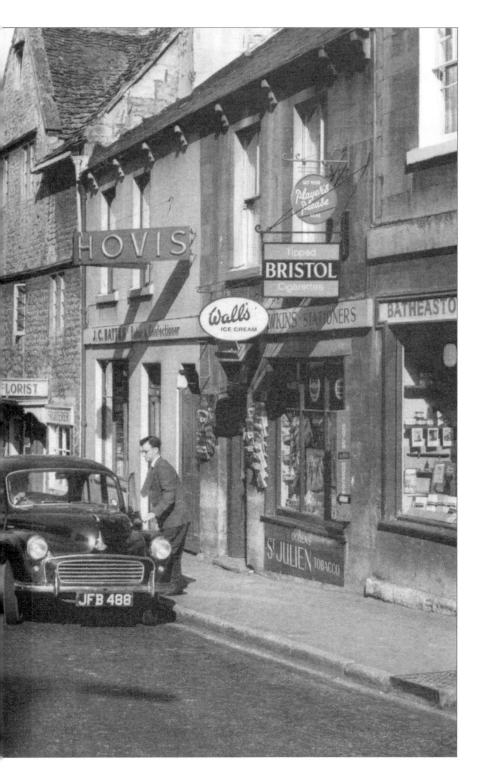

BATHEASTON
High Street c1960 B308019

The main road from London follows the Fosse Way here into Bath. Trams, originally horse-drawn, once ran along the same route. Down the street stands Batheaston House with its many chimneys: it was originally the home of the Walters family, 18th-century cloth merchants.

◄ **MONKTON COMBE**
General View c1955
M126015

In the centre of this picture are the buildings of Monkton Combe School. Beyond can be seen the Limpley Stoke viaduct, built for the Black Dog Turnpike Trust in 1834. A canal and railway passed under the bridge. To the right is Brassknocker Hill.

◀**BATHEASTON**
*Main Road and
the River c1965*
B308037

The Fosse Way runs
down from the
right of this picture
to meet the Avon
and follow it to
Bath, three miles
away. Mills grew
along the river and
St Catherine's
Brook producing
flour, leather, paper
and cloth, until the
brook was tapped
for water for Bath.

▲ **RADSTOCK,** *The Main Road c1965* R2035

In the 19th century this area was the centre of a busy coal mining industry. At the bottom of
Wells Hill we can see the railway station, which came with the Bath and Bristol line in 1874,
succeeding a canal and tramway for carrying coal. A busy weekly market stood by the crossing.

◀**FAULKLAND**
*The Faulkland Inn
c1960* F227003

Faulkland hamlet, in the
parish of Hemington,
declined with the end of
its coal mining industry.
Its 18th-century coaching
inn is of similar age to the
house of Thomas Turner,
who built a folly tower
nearby and shared with
the villagers his pond and
lawns, which became the
large village green.

FARLEIGH HUNGERFORD, *The Post Office c1960* F219011

Farleigh Hungerford's post office closed in the 1990s, but the village retains a school, a church and a pub. It is best known for its ruined castle, which once belonged to the Hungerford family, but it has also been popular for moto-cross and swimming in the River Frome.

INDEX

Frith Book Co Titles

www.francisfrith.co.uk

The Frith Book Company publishes over 100 new titles each year. A selection of those currently available is listed below. For latest catalogue please contact Frith Book Co.
Town Books 96 pages, approximately 100 photos. **County and Themed Books** 128 pages, approximately 150 photos (unless specified). All titles hardback with laminated case and jacket, except those indicated pb (paperback)

Amersham, Chesham & Rickmansworth (pb)	1-85937-340-2	£9.99	Devon (pb)	1-85937-297-x	£9.99
Andover (pb)	1-85937-292-9	£9.99	Devon Churches (pb)	1-85937-250-3	£9.99
Aylesbury (pb)	1-85937-227-9	£9.99	Dorchester (pb)	1-85937-307-0	£9.99
Barnstaple (pb)	1-85937-300-3	£9.99	Dorset (pb)	1-85937-269-4	£9.99
Basildon Living Memories (pb)	1-85937-515-4	£9.99	Dorset Coast (pb)	1-85937-299-6	£9.99
Bath (pb)	1-85937-419-0	£9.99	Dorset Living Memories (pb)	1-85937-584-7	£9.99
Bedford (pb)	1-85937-205-8	£9.99	Down the Severn (pb)	1-85937-560-x	£9.99
Bedfordshire Living Memories	1-85937-513-8	£14.99	Down The Thames (pb)	1-85937-278-3	£9.99
Belfast (pb)	1-85937-303-8	£9.99	Down the Trent	1-85937-311-9	£14.99
Berkshire (pb)	1-85937-191-4	£9.99	East Anglia (pb)	1-85937-265-1	£9.99
Berkshire Churches	1-85937-170-1	£17.99	East Grinstead (pb)	1-85937-138-8	£9.99
Berkshire Living Memories	1-85937-332-1	£14.99	East London	1-85937-080-2	£14.99
Black Country	1-85937-497-2	£12.99	East Sussex (pb)	1-85937-606-1	£9.99
Blackpool (pb)	1-85937-393-3	£9.99	Eastbourne (pb)	1-85937-399-2	£9.99
Bognor Regis (pb)	1-85937-431-x	£9.99	Edinburgh (pb)	1-85937-193-0	£8.99
Bournemouth (pb)	1-85937-545-6	£9.99	England In The 1880s	1-85937-331-3	£17.99
Bradford (pb)	1-85937-204-x	£9.99	Essex - Second Selection	1-85937-456-5	£14.99
Bridgend (pb)	1-85937-386-0	£7.99	Essex (pb)	1-85937-270-8	£9.99
Bridgwater (pb)	1-85937-305-4	£9.99	Essex Coast	1-85937-342-9	£14.99
Bridport (pb)	1-85937-327-5	£9.99	Essex Living Memories	1-85937-490-5	£14.99
Brighton (pb)	1-85937-192-2	£8.99	Exeter	1-85937-539-1	£9.99
Bristol (pb)	1-85937-264-3	£9.99	Exmoor (pb)	1-85937-608-8	£9.99
British Life A Century Ago (pb)	1-85937-213-9	£9.99	Falmouth (pb)	1-85937-594-4	£9.99
Buckinghamshire (pb)	1-85937-200-7	£9.99	Folkestone (pb)	1-85937-124-8	£9.99
Camberley (pb)	1-85937-222-8	£9.99	Frome (pb)	1-85937-317-8	£9.99
Cambridge (pb)	1-85937-422-0	£9.99	Glamorgan	1-85937-488-3	£14.99
Cambridgeshire (pb)	1-85937-420-4	£9.99	Glasgow (pb)	1-85937-190-6	£9.99
Cambridgeshire Villages	1-85937-523-5	£14.99	Glastonbury (pb)	1-85937-338-0	£7.99
Canals And Waterways (pb)	1-85937-291-0	£9.99	Gloucester (pb)	1-85937-232-5	£9.99
Canterbury Cathedral (pb)	1-85937-179-5	£9.99	Gloucestershire (pb)	1-85937-561-8	£9.99
Cardiff (pb)	1-85937-093-4	£9.99	Great Yarmouth (pb)	1-85937-426-3	£9.99
Carmarthenshire (pb)	1-85937-604-5	£9.99	Greater Manchester (pb)	1-85937-266-x	£9.99
Chelmsford (pb)	1-85937-310-0	£9.99	Guildford (pb)	1-85937-410-7	£9.99
Cheltenham (pb)	1-85937-095-0	£9.99	Hampshire (pb)	1-85937-279-1	£9.99
Cheshire (pb)	1-85937-271-6	£9.99	Harrogate (pb)	1-85937-423-9	£9.99
Chester (pb)	1-85937-382 8	£9.99	Hastings and Bexhill (pb)	1-85937-131-0	£9.99
Chesterfield (pb)	1-85937-378-x	£9.99	Heart of Lancashire (pb)	1-85937-197-3	£9.99
Chichester (pb)	1-85937-228-7	£9.99	Helston (pb)	1-85937-214-7	£9.99
Churches of East Cornwall (pb)	1-85937-249-x	£9.99	Hereford (pb)	1-85937-175-2	£9.99
Churches of Hampshire (pb)	1-85937-207-4	£9.99	Herefordshire (pb)	1-85937-567-7	£9.99
Cinque Ports & Two Ancient Towns	1-85937-492-1	£14.99	Herefordshire Living Memories	1-85937-514-6	£14.99
Colchester (pb)	1-85937-188-4	£8.99	Hertfordshire (pb)	1-85937-247-3	£9.99
Cornwall (pb)	1-85937-229-5	£9.99	Horsham (pb)	1-85937-432-8	£9.99
Cornwall Living Memories	1-85937-248-1	£14.99	Humberside (pb)	1-85937-605-3	£9.99
Cotswolds (pb)	1-85937-230-9	£9.99	Hythe, Romney Marsh, Ashford (pb)	1-85937-256-2	£9.99
Cotswolds Living Memories	1-85937-255-4	£14.99	Ipswich (pb)	1-85937-424-7	£9.99
County Durham (pb)	1-85937-398-4	£9.99	Isle of Man (pb)	1-85937-268-6	£9.99
Croydon Living Memories (pb)	1-85937-162-0	£9.99	Isle of Wight (pb)	1-85937-429-8	£9.99
Cumbria (pb)	1-85937-621-5	£9.99	Isle of Wight Living Memories	1-85937-304-6	£14.99
Derby (pb)	1-85937-367-4	£9.99	Kent (pb)	1-85937-189-2	£9.99
Derbyshire (pb)	1-85937-196-5	£9.99	Kent Living Memories(pb)	1-85937-401-8	£9.99
Derbyshire Living Memories	1-85937-330-5	£14.99	Kings Lynn (pb)	1-85937-334-8	£9.99

Available from your local bookshop or from the publisher

Frith Book Co Titles (continued)

Title	ISBN	Price	Title	ISBN	Price
Lake District (pb)	1-85937-275-9	£9.99	Sherborne (pb)	1-85937-301-1	£9.99
Lancashire Living Memories	1-85937-335-6	£14.99	Shrewsbury (pb)	1-85937-325-9	£9.99
Lancaster, Morecambe, Heysham (pb)	1-85937-233-3	£9.99	Shropshire (pb)	1-85937-326-7	£9.99
Leeds (pb)	1-85937-202-3	£9.99	Shropshire Living Memories	1-85937-643-6	£14.99
Leicester (pb)	1-85937-381-x	£9.99	Somerset	1-85937-153-1	£14.99
Leicestershire & Rutland Living Memories	1-85937-500-6	£12.99	South Devon Coast	1-85937-107-8	£14.99
Leicestershire (pb)	1-85937-185-x	£9.99	South Devon Living Memories (pb)	1-85937-609-6	£9.99
Lighthouses	1-85937-257-0	£9.99	South East London (pb)	1-85937-263-5	£9.99
Lincoln (pb)	1-85937-380-1	£9.99	South Somerset	1-85937-318-6	£14.99
Lincolnshire (pb)	1-85937-433-6	£9.99	South Wales	1-85937-519-7	£14.99
Liverpool and Merseyside (pb)	1-85937-234-1	£9.99	Southampton (pb)	1-85937-427-1	£9.99
London (pb)	1-85937-183-3	£9.99	Southend (pb)	1-85937-313-5	£9.99
London Living Memories	1-85937-454-9	£14.99	Southport (pb)	1-85937-425-5	£9.99
Ludlow (pb)	1-85937-176-0	£9.99	St Albans (pb)	1-85937-341-0	£9.99
Luton (pb)	1-85937-235-x	£9.99	St Ives (pb)	1-85937-415-8	£9.99
Maidenhead (pb)	1-85937-339-9	£9.99	Stafford Living Memories (pb)	1-85937-503-0	£9.99
Maidstone (pb)	1-85937-391-7	£9.99	Staffordshire (pb)	1-85937-308-9	£9.99
Manchester (pb)	1-85937-198-1	£9.99	Stourbridge (pb)	1-85937-530-8	£9.99
Marlborough (pb)	1-85937-336-4	£9.99	Stratford upon Avon (pb)	1-85937-388-7	£9.99
Middlesex	1-85937-158-2	£14.99	Suffolk (pb)	1-85937-221-x	£9.99
Monmouthshire	1-85937-532-4	£14.99	Suffolk Coast (pb)	1-85937-610-x	£9.99
New Forest (pb)	1-85937-390-9	£9.99	Surrey (pb)	1-85937-240-6	£9.99
Newark (pb)	1-85937-366-6	£9.99	Surrey Living Memories	1-85937-328-3	£14.99
Newport, Wales (pb)	1-85937-258-9	£9.99	Sussex (pb)	1-85937-184-1	£9.99
Newquay (pb)	1-85937-421-2	£9.99	Sutton (pb)	1-85937-337-2	£9.99
Norfolk (pb)	1-85937-195-7	£9.99	Swansea (pb)	1-85937-167-1	£9.99
Norfolk Broads	1-85937-486-7	£14.99	Taunton (pb)	1-85937-314-3	£9.99
Norfolk Living Memories (pb)	1-85937-402-6	£9.99	Tees Valley & Cleveland (pb)	1-85937-623-1	£9.99
North Buckinghamshire	1-85937-626-6	£14.99	Teignmouth (pb)	1-85937-370-4	£7.99
North Devon Living Memories	1-85937-261-9	£14.99	Thanet (pb)	1-85937-116-7	£9.99
North Hertfordshire	1-85937-547-2	£14.99	Tiverton (pb)	1-85937-178-7	£9.99
North London (pb)	1-85937-403-4	£9.99	Torbay (pb)	1-85937-597-9	£9.99
North Somerset	1-85937-302-x	£14.99	Truro (pb)	1-85937-598-7	£9.99
North Wales (pb)	1-85937-298-8	£9.99	Victorian & Edwardian Dorset	1-85937-254-6	£14.99
North Yorkshire (pb)	1-85937-236-8	£9.99	Victorian & Edwardian Kent (pb)	1-85937-624-X	£9.99
Northamptonshire Living Memories	1-85937-529-4	£14.99	Victorian & Edwardian Maritime Album (pb)	1-85937-622-3	£9.99
Northamptonshire	1-85937-150-7	£14.99	Victorian and Edwardian Sussex (pb)	1-85937-625-8	£9.99
Northumberland Tyne & Wear (pb)	1-85937-281-3	£9.99	Villages of Devon (pb)	1-85937-293-7	£9.99
Northumberland	1-85937-522-7	£14.99	Villages of Kent (pb)	1-85937-294-5	£9.99
Norwich (pb)	1-85937-194-9	£8.99	Villages of Sussex (pb)	1-85937-295-3	£9.99
Nottingham (pb)	1-85937-324-0	£9.99	Warrington (pb)	1-85937-507-3	£9.99
Nottinghamshire (pb)	1-85937-187-6	£9.99	Warwick (pb)	1-85937-518-9	£9.99
Oxford (pb)	1-85937-411-5	£9.99	Warwickshire (pb)	1-85937-203-1	£9.99
Oxfordshire (pb)	1-85937-430-1	£9.99	Welsh Castles (pb)	1-85937-322-4	£9.99
Oxfordshire Living Memories	1-85937-525-1	£14.99	West Midlands (pb)	1-85937-289-9	£9.99
Paignton (pb)	1-85937-374-7	£7.99	West Sussex (pb)	1-85937-607-x	£9.99
Peak District (pb)	1-85937-280-5	£9.99	West Yorkshire (pb)	1-85937-201-5	£9.99
Pembrokeshire	1-85937-262-7	£14.99	Weston Super Mare (pb)	1-85937-306-2	£9.99
Penzance (pb)	1-85937-595-2	£9.99	Weymouth (pb)	1-85937-209-0	£9.99
Peterborough (pb)	1-85937-219-8	£9.99	Wiltshire (pb)	1-85937-277-5	£9.99
Picturesque Harbours	1-85937-208-2	£14.99	Wiltshire Churches (pb)	1-85937-171-x	£9.99
Piers	1-85937-237-6	£17.99	Wiltshire Living Memories (pb)	1-85937-396-8	£9.99
Plymouth (pb)	1-85937-389-5	£9.99	Winchester (pb)	1-85937-428-x	£9.99
Poole & Sandbanks (pb)	1-85937-251-1	£9.99	Windsor (pb)	1-85937-333-x	£9.99
Preston (pb)	1-85937-212-0	£9.99	Wokingham & Bracknell (pb)	1-85937-329-1	£9.99
Reading (pb)	1-85937-238-4	£9.99	Woodbridge (pb)	1-85937-498-0	£9.99
Redhill to Reigate (pb)	1-85937-596-0	£9.99	Worcester (pb)	1-85937-165-5	£9.99
Ringwood (pb)	1-85937-384-4	£7.99	Worcestershire Living Memories	1-85937-489-1	£14.99
Romford (pb)	1-85937-319-4	£9.99	Worcestershire	1-85937-152-3	£14.99
Royal Tunbridge Wells (pb)	1-85937-504-9	£9.99	York (pb)	1-85937-199-x	£9.99
Salisbury (pb)	1-85937-239-2	£9.99	Yorkshire (pb)	1-85937-186-8	£9.99
Scarborough (pb)	1-85937-379-8	£9.99	Yorkshire Coastal Memories	1-85937-506-5	£14.99
Sevenoaks and Tonbridge (pb)	1-85937-392-5	£9.99	Yorkshire Dales	1-85937-502-2	£14.99
Sheffield & South Yorks (pb)	1-85937-267-8	£9.99	Yorkshire Living Memories (pb)	1-85937-397-6	£9.99

See Frith books on the internet at www.francisfrith.co.uk

FRITH PRODUCTS & SERVICES

Francis Frith would doubtless be pleased to know that the pioneering publishing venture he started in 1860 still continues today. Over a hundred and forty years later, The Francis Frith Collection continues in the same innovative tradition and is now one of the foremost publishers of vintage photographs in the world. Some of the current activities include:

Interior Decoration

Today Frith's photographs can be seen framed and as giant wall murals in thousands of pubs, restaurants, hotels, banks, retail stores and other public buildings throughout the country. In every case they enhance the unique local atmosphere of the places they depict and provide reminders of gentler days in an increasingly busy and frenetic world.

Product Promotions

Frith products are used by many major companies to promote the sales of their own products or to reinforce their own history and heritage. Frith promotions have been used by Hovis bread, Courage beers, Scots Porage Oats, Colman's mustard, Cadbury's foods, Mellow Birds coffee, Dunhill pipe tobacco, Guinness, and Bulmer's Cider.

Genealogy and Family History

As the interest in family history and roots grows world-wide, more and more people are turning to Frith's photographs of Great Britain for images of the towns, villages and streets where their ancestors lived; and, of course, photographs of the churches and chapels where their ancestors were christened, married and buried are an essential part of every genealogy tree and family album.

Frith Products

All Frith photographs are available Framed or just as Mounted Prints and Posters (size 23 x 16 inches). These may be ordered from the address below. From time to time other products - Address Books, Calendars, Table Mats, etc - are available.

The Internet

Already fifty thousand Frith photographs can be viewed and purchased on the internet through the Frith websites and a myriad of partner sites.

For more detailed information on Frith companies and products, look at these sites:

www.francisfrith.co.uk
www.francisfrith.com
(for North American visitors)

See the complete list of Frith Books at:

www.francisfrith.co.uk

This web site is regularly updated with the latest list of publications from the Frith Book Company. If you wish to buy books relating to another part of the country that your local bookshop does not stock, you may purchase on-line.

For further information, trade, or author enquiries please contact us at the address below:
The Francis Frith Collection, Frith's Barn, Teffont, Salisbury, Wiltshire, England SP3 5QP.
Tel: +44 (0)1722 716 376 Fax: +44 (0)1722 716 881 Email: sales@francisfrith.co.uk

See Frith books on the internet at www.francisfrith.co.uk